AMAZING OCEAN ANIMALS

DISCOVER THE WONDER OF THE OCEAN AND HOW WE CAN PROTECT IT

NOAH SAMUEL

AMAZING

OCEAN

ANIMALS

CONTENTS

THE BLUE PLANET

The sea covers 70% of the worlds surface and is divided into five main oceans. They are the Atlantic, Arctic, Indian, Pacific and Southern Ocean (Antarctica). The sea is so vast and deep we have only explored 20% of it. There is so much water on earth that it looks blue from space. This is why earth is called the 'Blue Planet'. Scientists have identified 230,000 different animal species in the oceans but believe that the total number is likely to be about 2,000,000 species.

The largest sea creature is the Blue whale. It can grow up to 33 metres long, the length of three buses! The smallest sea creatures are called micro-organisms and are so tiny that you would need a microscope to look at them. A tiny drop of water contains thousands of micro-organisms.

THE BLUE WHALE

The Blue whale is the largest sea mammal and weighs around 200 tonnes. Blue whales live in all the oceans, except for the Arctic. They migrate or travel, very long distances and their large mass helps them to survive these long journeys.

Despite their enormous body and mouth, these creatures are not predators. They do not even have teeth. They eat large amounts of small foods such as krill (little prawns). Instead of teeth they have brush like bristles called baleen plates that trap krill, small fish and plankton inside the whale's mouth whilst letting the water out at the same. This is known as filter feeding.

Blue whales give birth to live young, called calves, who stay with their mother for six or seven months. During this time, she provides milk for her young and keeps them safe from predators. The number of blue whales declined dramatically due to whaling but their numbers have slowly started to grow since they were protected in 1966.

BELUGA WHALE

Beluga whales live in the icy waters of the Arctic and reach about five metres in length. They are easily recognisable by their bright white colouring. Beluga whales live close to the shore and prey on small sea creatures. They have also been known to swim upstream in fresh water rivers looking for food. Beluga whales can dive into deep waters for up to 25 minutes at a time and can swim down as far as 1000 metres.

Beluga whales are well known for their expressive face and distinct chatter that includes whistles, clicks and squeals. Their facial expressions and song are made possible by their bulbous and stretchy forehead which is known as a 'melon'. Beluga whales are the only whale that can move their head from side to side as well as up and down. Beluga whales are mammals so they give birth to live young and care for them until they are grown.

ORCA

Orcas, also known as Killer whales, live in all the oceans of the world including Antarctica. Despite their nickname, Orca's are actually very large dolphins. They have black and white skin, a tall dorsal fin and are extremely intelligent. Orcas can grow to a length of ten metres. They are playful, curious and sociable and although they can be ferocious predators of sharks, seals and other prey, Orcas have never attacked humans in the wild.

Orcas live in social groups called pods. They adhere to social rules about behaviour, relationships and family life. They teach their young how to hunt and how to communicate using whale song and clicking sounds that are unique to each individual whale pod. These whale songs are passed down to younger generations.

Orcas are mammals so they are warm blooded and they give birth to live babies. They are extremely protective of their young who stay in their care for up to two years. Females can live to be 90 years old whilst males tend to live for about 60 years.

MANATEE

Manatees are herbivores (vegetarian) and are sometimes nick-named sea cows. Manatees are very gentle and don't have any predators, they spend their days grazing and slowly gliding through warm waters at about five miles an hour. They live on the coast line of the Caribbean, the Gulf of Mexico and on the west coast of Africa. Manatees are closely related to elephants.

Historical tales about Manatees date back to the 1500's, when they were often mistaken for mermaids. This is because of the way that Manatees slowly rise up from the water. They even stand on their hind tails the way that mermaids were imagined to do. From a distance they can look rather human and this was the source of many sailor's myths.

SEA TURTLE

Sea turtles lay their eggs on the same beach every season. They travel many miles to do this. Once there, they dig a hole several centimetres deep in which the eggs are laid. The turtle covers the eggs in sand using her fins before returning to the ocean.

Baby turtles take 50 to 80 days to hatch. They hatch in unison because they need a team effort to dig themselves out of the sand, which can take up to five days. Once out, they scurry quickly to the water's edge to take their first swim. When the turtles are grown, they return to the spot where they were born to lay their own eggs.

Turtles are reptiles. Reptiles are cold blooded animals and have dry, scaly skin. Turtles are ancient creatures that are believed to have lived alongside dinosaurs over 200 million years ago.

A turtle's shell is actually part of its body and it grows with them. The shell is made up of 50 bones and contains the spine and rib cage. Turtles use their shell to protect them from predators.

Turtles have beaks similar to birds, that clamp shut on prey. Turtles love to eat squid and jelly fish. The largest turtle was found in Wales in the UK. It was 2.5 metres long and weighed 900kg. Turtles can swim up to 20 miles a day and migrate (travel over long distances).

PENGUIN

There are 18 types of penguin. The largest is the Emperor Penguin which can grow four feet tall. Penguins mostly live in the southern hemisphere close to Antarctica but can also be found close to the equator. Penguins like to eat squid, krill and fish. They are birds but they are very good swimmers. Penguin's bodies are streamlined for swimming and their wings have adapted into flippers that act like propellers, allowing them to speed through the water at great speed.

Female penguins lay a single egg which is passed to the male for incubation (keeping it warm). He carries the egg between his legs and under a flap of skin for around 65 days, standing for the whole time in freezing temperatures of -40 degrees Celsius. When the fledgling is born the parents take turns to hunt for food for up to three weeks at a time. As the chicks grow up they herd into little groups called crèches. Penguin parents rear and their young in the harshest environment on earth.

SEA LION

Sea lions give birth to live babies called pups. They cannot breathe under water but are amazing swimmers that can free dive for up to 20 minutes at a time. Sea lions live in colonies and can grow to be ten feet long.

Seals and sea lions are alike but sea lions can use their flippers to walk on land. Like seals, sea lions communicate by barking and grunting both in and out of the water. They are very vocal, particularly when defending territory or trying to find a mate.

SEAL

There are 19 species of seal and they live in many different climates. The largest species is the Elephant Seal which grows to four metres long and can weigh two tonnes.

Seals spend most of their lives in the ocean but come ashore to gather on the beaches, bask in the sun and to mate and give birth to their pups. After giving birth, they shed a layer of their skin before returning to the water. Seals can hold their breath under water for up to two hours.

They eat fish, squid and jellyfish.

TROPICAL FISH

Tropical fish live in warm tropical environments and are most often found close to coral reefs. They live in both salt water and fresh water. Tropical fish adapt to their surroundings to protect themselves from predators. Their colours, movements and even their smell have adapted to act as camouflage. This has led to the evolution of some of the most fascinating and surprising creatures on the planet. Tropical fish have been demonstrated to have the capacity to learn and in captivity respond differently to different people especially if they are the one that provides the food!

WHITEMARGIN UNICORN FISH

Unicorn Fish live in the Indo-Pacific Ocean close to coral reef areas. They can grow to one metre in length. The (unicorn-like) horn on his snout is absent at birth but over time, it grows to about 13cm.

BOXFISH

Box Fish live in the Pacific, Indian and South-eastern Atlantic reefs. Their box-like shell is made of bony plates. When stressed they release a neurotoxin through the skin that poisons fish in its vicinity.

When afraid, blowfish blow themselves up to increase their size and protrude spikes from their body. Blowfish contain poison that can paralyse and kill but are also known for their cute faces and the way their eyes move independently of each other.

Pufferfish are closely related to Blowfish. They also fill their stretchy stomachs with large amounts of water to enlarge their body. Pufferfish are one of the most toxic creatures on earth. Their poison is 12,000 times more potent than cyanide.

The Butterfly Fish has a long snout and nose that it uses to forage food from the coral reefs it lives in. They have a false eye marking on their tails to confuse predators and their colourful stripes help them to camouflage against the reef.

Lionfish though beautiful, are one of the top predators of the coral reef. They eat around 50 types of fish and can lay 2,000,000 eggs in a year. Their colourful and poisonous spines mean they have no known predators. They have a very big mouth which they use to swallow their prey in one gulp.

Cowfish have horns on the front of their head that resemble the horns of a cow. When distressed they secrete a deadly poison through their skin to kill predators. Cowfish have an unusual way of swimming that makes them look like they are hovering in the water and not really moving.

Harlequin Filefish live on the coral reefs of the Indo-Pacific Ocean and are about 9cm in length.

They are known for their snout which secretes the smells of the coral they eat. This smell and their colour disguise them as coral so predators can't find them.

SEAHORSE

Seahorses don't swim. They float. They move up, down and sideways using four tiny fins. Every seahorse is different. Some seahorses have crowns, others have spines or frills. They can also change their colour to help them hide from predators.

To attract a mate, seahorses dance, entwine their tails together and change their colour multiple times to make themselves more attractive. Once mated, they stay together for a breeding season. Strangely, it is the male seahorse who becomes pregnant. Seahorses and sea dragons are the only species where the male has this ability.

OCTOPUS

Octopus prefer deep water and are famous for having eight long legs. They have a rounded head, bulging eyes and three hearts. The male must be careful during mating as the female sometimes eats her mate! She protects her eggs keenly, not even leaving them to eat. Not long after the eggs hatch, the female octopus will die.

Octopus are very clever and can solve complicated mazes and puzzles when tested by scientists. They have even been witnessed opening jars!

Octopus squirt black ink at predators as a deterrent when they feel threatened and though octopus are venomous to their prey, most octopus poisons will not harm humans.

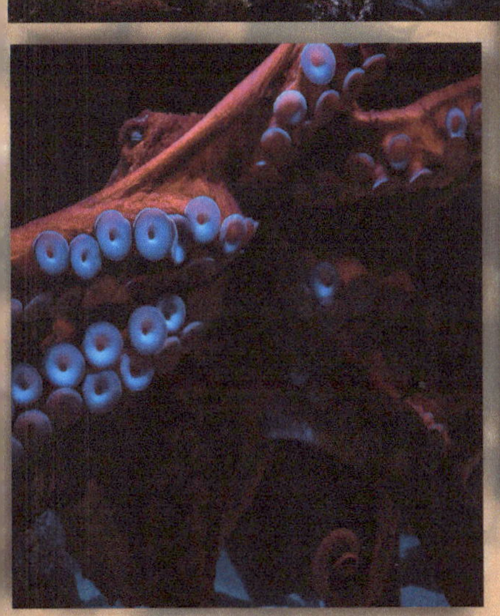

BLUE-RINGED OCTOPUS

Blue-ring octopus live in coral reefs in the Indian and Pacific Ocean and like to hide in caves. When they are stressed they change colour and this is a warning sign that they may attack. This warning should be heeded as the Blue-ringed octopus is one of the most venomous creatures on earth.

It is able to paralyse and kill an adult human with just one bite. Unfortunately, the bite is painless so a person would not know they had been bitten until paralysis sets in. This is extremely rare. There is no anti-venom for the poison but if treated immediately people have survived.

SHARK

Great white sharks are predatory fish and are around five metres long. They live about 70 years, in the coastal areas of all the oceans except Antarctica. Great white sharks do not have eye lids so they roll their eyes before an attack to protect them. Great whites smell blood in the water from three miles away and use electromagnetic fields to sense their prey. They are able jump 10 feet above the water and have five rows of teeth with 46 teeth in each row.

Tiger sharks can grow to five metres long and mostly live in the Pacific Ocean. They have stripes that fade with age and bristly, bony structures on their skin which sea creatures use as a brush to remove parasites – if they are brave enough to get that close!

Hammerhead sharks have 360-degree vision due to their eye placement. They live in groups called flocks but hunt alone at night. The Great Hammerhead can grow to six metres and is a ferocious hunter. They have even been known to eat their own kind.

Whale sharks are the largest fish, averaging 12 metres long. Despite this, whale sharks are filter feeders and only eat tiny foods like plankton.

Whale sharks migrate long distances to warm waters and are particularly fond of Mexico! Whale sharks lay and incubate eggs inside their body. When they hatch, the shark gives birth to live young

BOTTLENOSE DOLPHIN

Bottlenose dolphins live in all the oceans except the Arctic and the Antarctic. They are considered to be the most intelligent animal species on the planet after humans. Dolphins live in groups called pods and abide by mating and hunting rituals. They communicate using pulses of sound, whistles, squeaks, squeals and long tones. Dolphins communicate to be social and also, to express their emotional state. Dolphins sometimes blow air out of their blow hole to indicate that they are happy and want to play.

Dolphins warn each other when predators are close by frantically whistling to their companions. Dolphins are able to organise themselves to escape dangerous situations and this ability to co-operate with each other has ensured their survival.

STINGRAY

Stingrays are closely related to sharks. They are flat fish with very wide fins that give them a rounded diamond shape similar to a kite. Stingrays have no bones in their body, only bendy soft cartilage (the same as sharks). They are extremely graceful and glide or fly through the water.

Stingrays do not have teeth but they do have a very long tail with a barb or stinger at the end. This pointy barb is venomous and is often used to spear their prey. A Stingray's flat body is ideal for hiding in the sand. They spend most of their time on the seabed scavenging for crustaceans to eat. Stingrays like to eat prawns, krill, snails, clams and crabs. Like sharks, stingrays have electrical sensors in their mouth which help them to detect their prey.

Stingrays are cold blooded and lay eggs which they keep in a pouch inside them, until they hatch. The pockets in which they store their eggs is sometimes called a 'mermaids' purse'. They will then give birth to about thirteen babies called 'pups'.

CRAB

Crabs are ancient creatures that lived alongside dinosaurs. Crabs are crustaceans which means that their skeleton is worn on the outside. It is called an exoskeleton. Crabs can be very small or very large. The largest crab found was a Spider crab and measured 12 feet wide (not including his legs).

Most crabs live on the shore and enjoy rock pools and small rocky crevices which they can squeeze themselves into. They swim and walk sideways and they eat both meat and plants.

THE SEA

The sea is essential to the survival of our planet. Just like humans need water to drink, the world needs water to sustain it. The sea not only provides food for humans, it also creates the air we breathe and the water we drink. The sea even controls the weather by absorbing heat and transporting it around the world using ocean currents.

The ocean and everything in it, are all part of an enormous ecosystem. An ecosystem is an interactive environment made up of living and non-living things. Plants, animals, corals and plankton are all parts of ecosystems. All of these different elements work together to keep our oceans healthy by providing food and safe habitats for life to thrive. When an element of an ecosystem is removed or damaged, the rest of the ecosystem has to adapt.

If it cannot, animals and plants that once flourished can die because they don't have the environments or food supply they need to survive.

GLOBAL WARMING

The temperature of the earth is rising due to global warming. As the planet gets warmer, ecosystems are changing. Changes in weather can lead to more droughts, floods and forest fires. Animals have to find new places to live and new food sources.

Global warming happens when gases (called carbon dioxide) are caught in the earth's atmosphere very close to space. These trapped gases stop heat from escaping causing what is known as the 'greenhouse effect'. We call it the greenhouse effect because the gases create a barrier causing the planet to retain heat, much in the same way as glass windows retain heat in a greenhouse.

The sea plays a big part in the fight against global warming because it is able to absorb carbon dioxide. Taking care of the sea means that the sea can take care of us too.

CORAL REEF

Changes to the sea's temperature has a negative impact on the coral reef. More than 25% of all marine life relies on the coral reef for survival. It is the rainforest of the sea. Since the 1950's, we have lost more than half of our coral reefs. If things don't improve the children of today may be the last generation to experience it. This is due to global warming, over fishing and pollution. Coral is very sensitive to subtle changes. When the water is too warm the coral expels algae which causes the water to become more acidic. This is called bleaching. If this happens too often the coral reef turns white and dies and sea creatures have less places to hide, mate and feed.

OVER FISHING

Over fishing is when people and companies take too many fish from the sea. This is a big problem for marine life. Over the last 40 years nearly 40% of marine species have disappeared from our oceans.

Many animals and fish such as dolphins, turtles and stingrays are caught by mistake in the enormous fishing nets that are dragged along the ocean bed. Sadly, these creatures often die and are discarded as waste.

PLASTIC POLLUTION

Every year tonnes of rubbish and plastic is thrown into the oceans. Right now, there are more than five trillion pieces of plastic in the sea and this number increases every year. By 2050, there will be more pieces of plastic in the sea than there are fish.

Plastic does not bio degrade (waste away naturally). Once in the sea, plastic just stays there causing chaos to the eco- system and marine life. Plastic bags can look surprisingly similar to jellyfish when you are a turtle. Many animals die eating rubbish that they thought was a tasty snack.

Plastic breaks down into a powdery substance called micro plastic. It looks a little like white sand. These tiny particles absorb toxins and chemicals and are poisonous when eaten.

Micro plastics have been found in plankton which are a major source of food for marine life. The small fish eat these tiny particles, the bigger fish eat the tiny fish, and the really big fish eat the bigger fish! Micro plastics cause disease and can impact reproductive abilities meaning that the numbers of sea creatures are decreasing. The whole food chain is impacted.

ENERGY

Energy is used to heat our homes; to grow, prepare and cook food. We use energy to make clothes and products that we use every day and to light and power our homes and vehicles. Every time we switch on or plug in, we use energy.

89% of the energy we rely on comes from fossil fuels like coal, oil and gas. These types of energy release huge amounts of carbon into the atmosphere. Very clever humans are working on new ways to develop alternative, greener ways to provide our energy using wind farms, solar power and renewable energies like electricity that don't run out and don't affect our atmosphere. Next time you are powering up think about where your energy comes from and if you can reduce the amount you use. Is there a more environmentally friendly way you can achieve your goal?

Talk to grown-ups about renewable energy and protecting the environment.

Walk or ride a bike instead of taking the car.

Unplug devices when you aren't using them.

Check out how products are made, packaged and transported. Buy fresh, buy local and buy things that use less processes to make.

Don't turn up the heat, put on a cosy jumper!

Only cook, eat and heat what you need. Wasting food, heat and water wastes energy.

Turn off the lights and heating in empty rooms.

Always throw away your rubbish. Make sure you recycle as much as you can.

Join a beach clean-up or get involved in an eco-friendly project.

Buy loose fruit and vegetables - avoid plastic packets.

Take care of your things and make them last. Buying new items rather than fixing old ones can create more waste that may need to be buried or burnt.

Buy dolphin friendly tuna and fish that has been caught sustainably.

Save water. Spend less time in the shower, don't over fill the kettle and turn off the tap when you brush your teeth.

Use products sold in bio-degradable or refillable packaging.

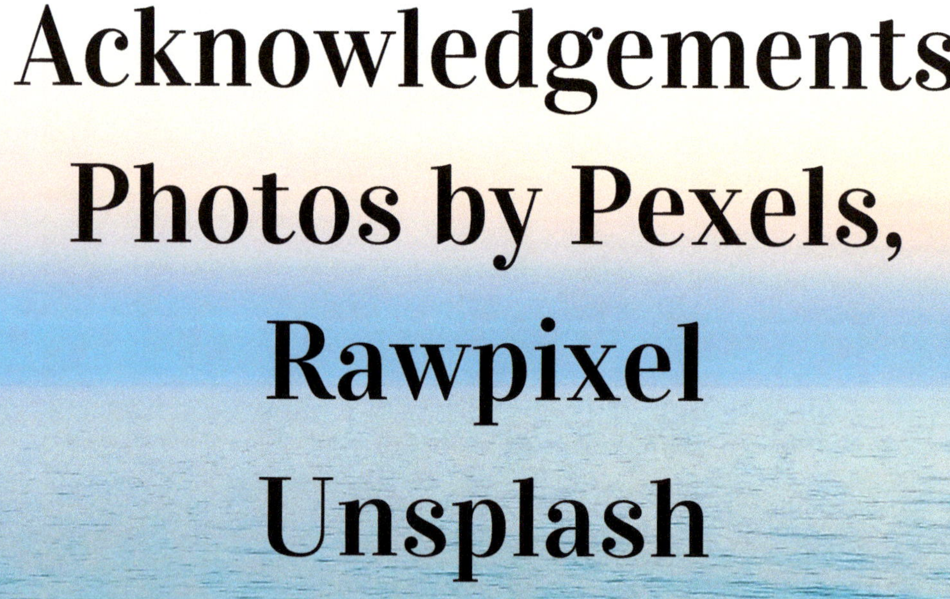

Acknowledgements

Photos by Pexels,

Rawpixel

Unsplash

EXPLORE THE WONDERS OF THE OCEAN AND MEET SOME OF OUR FAVOURITE SEA CREATURES INCLUDING SEA TURTLES, SHARKS, FISH, DOLPHINS AND PENGUINS. RICH WITH FACTS AND INFORMATION ABOUT WHAT MAKES OCEAN ANIMALS TRULY AMAZING AND STUNNING MARINE PHOTOGRAPHY THAT BRINGS THE ANIMALS TO LIFE.

LEARN WHY OUR OCEANS AND WILDLIFE ARE SO IMPORTANT AND HOW CHANGES TO THE EARTHS ENVIRONMENT IMPACTS THEM. CONSIDER WHAT YOU CAN DO TO HELP PROTECT OUR BEAUTIFUL OCEAN HABITATS. A BOOK THE WHOLE FAMILY CAN ENJOY.